New Island / New Drama

Long Black Coat

In the same series:

A Night in November — Marie Jones

LONG BLACK COAT

John Waters
(with David Byrne)

New Island Books / Dublin
Nick Hern Books / London

Long Black Coat
is first published in 1995
in Ireland by
New Island Books,
2, Brookside,
Dundrum Road,
Dublin 14
Ireland
& in Britain by
Nick Hern Books,
14 Larden Road,
London W3 7ST.

ISBN   1 874597 22 7 (New Island Books)
          1 85459 263 7 (Nick Hern Books)

New Island Books receives financial assistance from
The Arts Council (An Chomhairle Ealaíon),
Dublin, Ireland.

Cover design by Jon Berkeley
Cover photo of Seán Ó Tárpaigh as Jody by Tom Brett
Typeset by Graphic Resources
Printed in Ireland by Colour Books, Ltd.

Long Black Coat was first produced by **Bickerstaffe Theatre** Company at Cleere's Theatre, Kilkenny, in August, 1994. The cast was as follows:

OLD MAN	Kevin Flood
JODY	Seán Ó Tárpaigh
VISITOR	Denis Conway
Director	David Byrne
Co-producers	Richard Cook
	Lynn Cahill
Design	Paki Smith

ACT ONE

A large room, decorated ambiguously in terms of past and future. There is, centre back stage, a window completely obscured by a wardrobe, half-filled with earth. The doors of the wardrobe are closed. Inside the wardrobe a man's black coat is hanging, half-buried in the earth. Actors' right of the wardrobe, against the side wall, is a half-constructed lean-to shelter, built of doors and lengths of timber, and piled high outside with household objects. At the other side of the room is a table, beside which are a number of earth-filled drawers, surrounded by piles of books. There is a door actors' left, leading off stage to a hallway. In the corner of the room is a helmet-style apparatus on a stand — a Virtual Reality Helmet, which has the appearance of an insect's head. The helmet is actually a somewhat outmoded piece of technology, which does not function properly. Reception is erratic, and the transmission is received in fits and starts, giving the sense that the helmet has a life of its own. This malfunction is in fact due to an unspecified intermittent fault in the apparatus. The Old Man's armchair is actors' right of wardrobe. Otherwise the room contains the usual things: an old record player, and two or three other chairs. There are several boxes, general bric-a-brac, and a pile of tinned food on the floor. There is also a button accordion. There are two clocks in the room, one over the lean-to and the other on the opposite wall.

The Old Man is in his mid-60s. A fastidious, authoritative man, the house belongs to him. Jody, his "son", is in his early 30s, and has returned home to visit, having lived away for a number of years. Within the house, their relationship is that of adult and child. The house is at the end of a quiet street on the periphery of a small town.

7

(The OLD MAN *sits in the lean-to, with a fistful of pieces of cardboard, carefully clipped from cigarette boxes.* JODY *enters with a barrowful of clay. He is listening to a walkman.)*

JODY: D'ya think we'll have enough in this? There's a right hole out there now.

OLD MAN: Maybe another barrowful.

JODY: What's that?

OLD MAN: Maybe another barrowful.

JODY: What?

(OLD MAN *stops and looks at him.* JODY *removes the walkman.)*

OLD MAN: There's a few more drawers upstairs. Better bring them down and fill them while you're at it. The wardrobe'll take all you have there and more.

JODY: I'm making tea. Will you have some?

OLD MAN: Are you leaving that there? (JODY *continues walking away.)* I said are you leaving that there? Or maybe you're planning to put a tablecloth on it.

JODY: I'm spittin' feathers with all that dust.

OLD MAN: Look, you'll have plenty of time to be drinkin' tea when the job is finished. Finish what you're at before you start anything else. (JODY *begins to shovel soil into wardrobe.* OLD MAN *watches him closely.)* It's no use if it's just thrown in. You should be packin' it down well. You want to have it solid, nearly like concrete.

JODY: Ya, ya, ya. Don't you worry. The job is oxo.

OLD MAN: Let me show you there. *(Takes shovel from* JODY.*)*

OLD MAN: Ah, Jesus Christ! What do you think you're doing?

(The OLD MAN *has looked inside wardrobe for the first time and seen his coat half buried in clay.)*

JODY: What? What now? What have I done now?

OLD MAN: What have you done? Jesus Christ! Is there no end to it?

JODY: What's wrong with you now?

OLD MAN: What's wrong with me? What? Me coat. That's what's wrong with me. Me good feckin' coat. Ah Jesus Christ. Me good coat. It's destroyed. Have you any shaggin' head on you at all?

JODY: Your good coat. You haven't worn that coat in ten years. Sure the moths have it riddled.

OLD MAN: I only wore it the once or twice.

JODY: If you had any mass on it, it's not hangin up there it'd be for the moths and maggots to be fattening themselves on. Good coat!

OLD MAN: A man has to have a good coat. You never know when you might need it. Have you any idea how much a coat like that'd cost you today?

JODY: Jesus, if you're so fond of it, why don't you wear it?

OLD MAN: I put it away there for special occasions. And now it's destroyed. I'll have to wait until that clay dries out. Is there a clothes brush itself to be found in this place?

JODY: Yourself and your coat. Going round the place like a feckin' preacher man. A long coat and a longer face.

OLD MAN: The job is oxo! You could pack a ton more soil in here. You'll want another half-dozen barrowfuls at least. It's no bloody good unless its packed in tight. We're not trying to grow anything here, you know!

JODY: That's for sure.

(Relenting somewhat, the OLD MAN *bends down, picks a handful of soil from the heap on the floor.)*

OLD MAN: That's good ould soil all the same.

JODY: Is it?

OLD MAN: Oh yes. Good hearted soil. Lovely texture. Just the right mix. Oh yes. Do you know the ingredients of good soil?

JODY: Hmmph?

OLD MAN: Sand, humus and clay. The humus is the most important ingredient, you know. Plants live, first and foremost, on the remains of their ancestors. It should break down into crumbs, like bread. See? But that's not much good for this job here. You want it well packed down for this job.

JODY: It must've been all that digging I did when I was small.

OLD MAN: What?

JODY: The clay. It must be all the digging I did that made it so healthy, so "good-hearted".

OLD MAN: Digging? Digging? You never did much diggin' that I can remember.

JODY: I spent months out in that garden when I was a young fella. D'ya not remember when you used to have me out diggin' for worms? Every Thursday morning, when yourself and Mattie Barrett used to go off fishin' down to the swallyhole? You used to give me a pound to dig worms. And get the garden dug into the bargain!

OLD MAN: Worms. Did you ever hear that if you have enough worms in your garden you don't have to dig it at all? Oh no. It's better to leave it alone. The worms'll shift about a ton of soil in a year. A good gardener will leave the worms to do the business as much as possible.

JODY: Right. So what you're tellin' me now is what? That I shouldn't have dug the garden at all, but let the worms get on with the job. Could you just fill me in on the correct procedure, because I'm sort of a bit unclear.

OLD MAN: Ahh, enough of your ould lip.

JODY: And how would you see yourself now, as a gardener or a fisherman?

OLD MAN: Ah, sure there's neither fishermen nor gardeners to be had now. People are too lazy to scratch themselves. *(He examines the inside of the wardrobe.)* That soil is a bit damp all the same.

JODY: No!

OLD MAN: You should have lined that thing with paper or something before you started.

JODY: No.

OLD MAN: What?

JODY: If you want me to fill it up with shite, I'll fill it up with shite. But I'm not wallpaperin' it first. You can put that out of your mind.

OLD MAN: That's a good wardrobe. You wouldn't buy the like of that now.

JODY: This is the end of a glittering career. It'll be shag all use to anyone after this.

OLD MAN: When this thing is all over, you'll have to empty it and let it air out in the back garden. If you think I'm throwing out a good wardrobe like that you better think again.

JODY: Well, I hope we're all around to be worried about the state of the wardrobe, that's all I can say. Are you sure this is what we're supposed to do anyway?

OLD MAN: The booklet is over here. *(Moves towards lean-to.)*

JODY: It's pure fucken daft.

OLD MAN: You can read it for yourself. The windows have to be blocked out completely, it says.

JODY: But sure won't the shutters do that.

OLD MAN: They're no good. *(Reading from booklet.)* You have to have at least the thickness of the walls. It says here that you can use a wardrobe to shield a window...so long as the clay is packed down well. *(He skip-reads.)* "Windows and doors give hardly any protection. The windows and any outside doors of the room will have to be shielded when you take cover. This also applies to inside doors if they are not already shielded by thick walls...You can block windows and doors in one or more of these ways: One, by building up a barricade of bricks or concrete blocks outside the window (or inside if the floor will take the weight). It should be about equal to the wall thickness." I wonder what's the latest news about all this caper?

JODY: Can't you switch it on there and find out?

OLD MAN: I'm not going near that yoke.

JODY: What's it for so?

OLD MAN: It's a wonder it hasn't blown the place up before now.

JODY: Jesus, where did you put that remote? *(He begins searching round the room.)*

OLD MAN: You wouldn't catch me with that yoke on me head. I don't know what was wrong with the ould box in the corner.

JODY: Sure what's the point in havin' it so?

OLD MAN: 3-D Beamer! Virtual Reality. Unreality. No wonder the world is upside down. (JODY *continues to search.*) D'ya know, I can remember where I was the first time I saw a television. I was only a young fellah. Short trousers. We never heard of it. At least I hadn't. We didn't even have a wireless. Not one that worked at any rate. My father had a dozen of them in the attic, but none of them worked. And I was hungry for talk, for music. Then one day, I heard this word on the street. No. I heard three words. Tell. A. Vision. I knew what a vision was: it was when Our Lady appeared to Saint Bernadette. I read the book, **The Song of Bernadette**. I thought it would be a special kind of radio. I seen a crowd of people gathering outside the window of Jimmy Clarke's radio shop. He was an ould fellah that could fix anything. Sparks, they called him. Sparks Clarke is a gen-us they used to say. I looked around at the faces. They were fixed on the window. I couldn't understand what they were looking at for so long. Then, out of the corner of my eye, I saw something move over up high in the corner of the shop. It wasn't a radio they were looking at. It was this other box on a shelf. I saw a ship moving through snow. That's all I remember. A ship moving through snow. I know now it wasn't real snow. Interference. You'd see more in the fire. That's the first thing I remember about it. Tell. A. Vision. It seems like a thousand years ago. (JODY *has located the remote control and points it at the headset. Nothing happens.*)

JODY: And maybe it was.

OLD MAN: What's that?

JODY: Nothing. What time is it anyway?

OLD MAN: I can't see. What time is it on the clock there?

JODY: *(Looking at clock on wall.)* Quarter to six. Ah Jesus. It must be well after seven now. Christ almighty! It's impossible to find out a simple thing like the time of day in this place.

OLD MAN: Can you not go in and look at the clock in the kitchen?

JODY: Sure the clocks in this house are all arseways. Every clock has a different time. I never know what time it is. That clock there. Is it fast or slow?

OLD MAN: You're long enough around the place now to know that.

JODY: I was supposed to be making a phone call around six. Why can't you have clocks that work the same way as everyone else's?

OLD MAN: Because it suits me the way it is. That's why. It's not too hard to work out. How is it I'm able to know what time it is?

JODY: That clock in the kitchen is — what? — half an hour slow?

OLD MAN: An hour and three-quarters fast.

JODY: And the clock in the hall?

OLD MAN: An hour and a quarter.

JODY: Fast?

OLD MAN: Slow.

JODY: And the one on the landing?

OLD MAN: Three quarters.

JODY: Slow?

OLD MAN: Fast. Aren't you looking at it every day of the week?

JODY: And that clock there? *(Points to clock over lean-to.)*

OLD MAN: I told you a hundred times. That one is an hour and a half slow. It's very straightforward. The right time is halfway between that clock there and the one on the landing. *(Indicates clock on wall.)*

JODY: But it's stopped. What the fuck time is it in this friggin' house?

OLD MAN: If it stops it won't start up again on its own. You have to re-set it and jump-start it with the switch on the side.

JODY: Jesus, it must be after six. I better make that phone-call.

OLD MAN: It's not phoning you should be. It's above with your family you should be at a time like this.

JODY: And who'd look after you?

OLD MAN: I'm well able to look after meself. It's your family need looking after.

JODY: They're well looked after, don't you worry.

(Phone rings. OLD MAN waits for JODY, who refuses to move. OLD MAN, in exasperation, picks it up.)

OLD MAN: Hello. Who's speaking? Hello. Oh, howya Pet? Are ye well? Good, good. Oh sudden times. Sudden times. Don't ye be worrying. We overed worse in our day. Yes. Yes. Hold on. You're wanting here.

JODY: Who is it?

OLD MAN: Your wife. Who d'ya think it is?

JODY: Oh. Right. Hello. I'm sorry. The clocks in this place...How is he? How's Dylan? Yeah good. Yeah well. Oh yeah. It's like World War Three in this place. What? Oh. Yeah, I suppose that's what it is. Listen, have you made your mind up yet? About Dylan. Can he come over? I've got the place ready for him. I'm makin' a kind of an igloo for him under the table. He'll be as snug as a bug...He's my son too. Yeah, okay. Can I talk to him? Can I talk to Dylan? Yeah. Right. Dylan? Hullo boss!

OLD MAN: Hello Dylan.

JODY: Grandad says Hello. Are ya alright? Good lad. Good lad. You have your bed made up? Under the table? And your tent? Good man! You'll keep an eye on your mammy now, won't ya. You're the man of the house now. The man of the house. No, you are. No he is not. Alright? Good lad. Can you put mammy back on? Good lad. Hello. If you have any problems, you can give me a ring. Okay. Goodnight. Say goodnight to him, won't ya? *(Goes to hang up, then thinks of something.)* Pat? Pat? Are you still there? Pat? *(No answer. He hangs up dejectedly.)*

OLD MAN: Can't you ring her back?

JODY: Ah no. It's nothing. It can wait.

OLD MAN: Pick up that phone and ring the girl back.

JODY: No, it's all right. I'll talk to her tomorrow.

OLD MAN: Tomorrow. Hah! Tomorrow. That's a good one. This is not your place at a time like this. You should be up there with your wife and your son.

JODY: Lookit. Leave it.

OLD MAN: I'm just speaking the truth.

JODY: Look, fuck the truth. She's not my...Just...just leave it.

OLD MAN: That's a nice way to speak to your father...

JODY: Me father. Hah? Now that is a good one.

(JODY *exits.* OLD MAN *makes to sit down, picks up accordion which is on the ground nearby, and looks for someplace to put it. Then, remembering, he plays a couple of bars of 'The Dawning of the Day'. He then puts it in the buggy and wheels it once around the room.* JODY *enters with a toilet bowl, drops it in the middle of the floor and sits on it.*)

OLD MAN: In the name of God where are you going with that?

JODY: I'm goin' to put a tablecloth on it.

OLD MAN: Sure that's no use. You need a water supply.

JODY: Even if we never use it, won't you feel comfortable havin' it beside you.

OLD MAN: What?

JODY: In my father's house there are many mansions.

OLD MAN: What are you goin' on about?

JODY: To smoke your fags, read your paper and work on your sermons.

OLD MAN: Sure I haven't smoked a fag in twenty years.

JODY: But you're still talkin' shite.

OLD MAN: What's that? What'd you say?

JODY: I was just sayin' it was screwed down shockin' tight.

OLD MAN: Put that thing back where you found it.

JODY: Wouldn't it be a terror if you were caught short! We've an awful lot of beans to get through.

OLD MAN: And I suppose you intend to sink a septic tank in the corner as well.

JODY: But you'll need somewhere to go.

OLD MAN: I have that organised.

JODY: I thought you might all right.

OLD MAN: I fixed up a chemical loo under the stairs while you were feckin' about with a few shovelfuls of clay.

JODY: Oh sure you'd be lost without your inner sanctum — to ruminate and fabricate and get your stories straight.

OLD MAN: Put that back where you found it, and don't be actin the lug.

(Banging on outside door. They stop what they're doing and remain silent, pretending they're not in. Banging ceases. They look at one another.)

JODY: Maybe the alert's gone off...

OLD MAN: *(With remote control in his hand.)* Would there be any news on that yoke? *(Gestures towards Virtual Reality device.)*

JODY: *(Takes remote control.)* Sure that feckin' thing won't stay on a station most of the time. You'd get more news on this yoke here. *(Indicates toilet bowl.)* It's coming on.

(Loud explosion from Virtual Reality headset.)

OLD MAN: Coming on? I'm off! Sure the feckin things'd frighten the living daylights outa you. Splutterin' and buzzin' and fartin'.

JODY: Will you not get a new one? This thing is out of the ark.

OLD MAN: Oh Jesus. Stand back from that thing before you hurt yourself.

MALE PRESENTER: *(Signal is occasionally broken up by static.)* The Prime Minister told a press conference that the strength of our resolve at this hour of danger would be the measure of the spirit of the times. We must wipe from the honour of our civilisation the dark stain of the evil which now threatens to engulf it, she said. We are engaged in a struggle between good and evil. *(Static.)* Future generations would come in pilgrimage to the places where Western Civilisation was saved from the darkness of infamy. We must stand firm, she said, in defence of the integrity of our ways, the values of our civilisation, the character of our convictions and the decency of our traditions.

FEMALE PRESENTER: Meanwhile, a spokesman for the Aya-tollah said that the people of his country were the victims of a campaign of demonisation by Western imperialists. Our citizens are peace-loving people, he said. *(Static.)* We have this big army, these weapons of destruction, so that no one can come and tweak our moustaches or pull our beards, and so that we can cut off the hand that tries to do this. *(Static.)* Suns will rise, moons will shine and the stars will glitter.

MALE PRESENTER: And that's the update this hour. I'm Bill Cleary.

FEMALE PRESENTER: And I'm Jane Maxwell. Thanks Bill. The weather outlook this hour... *(Transmission begins to break up.)*

JODY: Ah Jesus. *(Shifts the aerial about. Transmission comes and goes through the following exchanges.)*

FEMALE PRESENTER: Outlook is for slightly improved weather over the weekend...Dry again tomorrow with further sunshine. So the medium term outlook is for dry, settled weather. Bill?

OLD MAN: Would ya get up the yard. Did you ever hear the like? Medium term outlook?

MALE PRESENTER: Well, Jane, hope we're all still around to enjoy that nice spell of weather.

FEMALE PRESENTER: Yes indeed Bill. I could do with a stint in the back garden to top up my tan.

OLD MAN: Ye'll be well tanned if you go out tomorrow.

MALE PRESENTER: Looks pretty good from here! But if you want the latest update on the prospects for tomorrow...stay tuned to this channel for more live updates from the crisis centre. Right now we're joining our reporter in a helicopter overlooking the battle centre.

JODY: A helicopter. I must have a look at this. *(He picks up the helmet.)*

OLD MAN: It's not going up in a helicopter you should be. It's above with your family you should be.

JODY: Just leave it. D'ya hear?

OLD MAN: I'm only saying that you should try and make it up with the girl. That's all I'm sayin'. You should never have left that girl.

JODY: Just leave it, will you. *(He puts the helmet on his head.)*

OLD MAN: Virtual Reality. Yourself and your 3-D Beamer. Try stickin' your head into the real world for a change.

(JODY *takes the helmet off and glares at* OLD MAN.)

JODY: Will you just leave it.

OLD MAN: All I'm sayin' is that she's your wife. You never should've left her.

JODY: I didn't leave her. It was her decision. I had no say in the matter.

OLD MAN: Well, you should try a bit harder to get back in there. She's a nice girl.

JODY: What do you know about her?

OLD MAN: I know enough to know she's a cut above the rest. She's the mother of your child. You were happy enough to go along with that part of it.

JODY: I couldn't keep up with her. All she was after was me body. *(Goes to put helmet on.)*

OLD MAN: What are you saying?

JODY: Once she was pregnant she couldn't wait to see the back of me.

OLD MAN: Maybe she could see what a weakling you are.

JODY: Did you ever hear about what happens to the male red-backed spider?

OLD MAN: Hah?

JODY: When he's finished the business to the satisfaction of her ladyship, she kills him, trusses him up and puts him away to make sandwiches for the youngsters when they arrive. That's me.

OLD MAN: I never saw any sign of that on her. You must have done something on the girl.

JODY: What d'you know about her?

OLD MAN: Anyway, what's done is done. Now you have to face up to your responsibilities.

JODY: What d'ya mean, Face up to my responsibilities?

OLD MAN: Do you want to be a father to your son, or do you want to be acting the child for the rest of your life?

JODY: Of course I want to be a father to him. D'ya not think it's burning me up every minute of the day, that I'm not with him, that I can't see his face. See him smile at me. D'ya not think I care.

OLD MAN: You tell me. The point of parents is that they're in it together.

JODY: Not any more. Maybe in your day, yeah. But it doesn't have to be like that these days.

OLD MAN: My day. Your day. These days. It doesn't matter what day it is if you're the child in the middle of it. That boy has only one set of parents, and God help him, you're half of it.

JODY: Between her trying to turn me into her father and you trying to turn me into you, I don't know whether I'm coming or going. *(He puts helmet on. And takes it off again immediately.)*

OLD MAN: Yeah, yeah, yeah.

JODY: Chip, chip, chip, the whole day long, 'til there's nothing left of who you even think you might be.

OLD MAN: Yeah, yeah, yeah.

JODY: If I don't do what she wants I'm damned for being wicked, and if I do I'm damned for being weak. Her goin' round the place with her faces, sighs, silences. Then tears.

(In exasperation, JODY *puts helmet on his head.)*

OLD MAN: Jesus, you look like the bloody man in the moon with that thing on you.

JODY: *(Takes off helmet.)* What?

OLD MAN: You look like the bloody man in the moon with that thing on you. One small step for man. One giant leap for mankind.

JODY: That's *a man*.

OLD MAN: What?

JODY: One small step for *a man*. One giant leap for mankind. He said *a man*.

OLD MAN: No he didn't.

JODY: Yes he did.

OLD MAN: No.

JODY: We did it in school. He said "One small step for *a man*. One small step for man doesn't make sense.

OLD MAN: Yes it does.

JODY: No, it doesn't. *A man*. It's what's in the history books.

OLD MAN: Didn't I hear it a hundred times. On the recording. One small step for man. That's what he said.

JODY: No it wasn't. He said "One small step for *a man*..." Only the "a" was lost in transmission.

OLD MAN: No. I was there.

JODY: They were using a voice-activated system. It was called Vox. It can lose a syllable every so often. *(Puts on helmet.)*

OLD MAN: I was there. I remember. Well, not there. We had no television. But I remember. The whole town was caught up in it. Not a sinner on the street. Ghost-town. I used to watch television sometime in the house next door. The day of the moon landing, they had visitors. A cousin getting ordained. I missed the landing. But I was there. I climbed a tree instead. Just at the moment they walked on to the moon. I climbed the big sycamore tree at the end of our garden. The first time. I got to the very top. I looked all around at the still countryside. Magnificent desolation. The next day I did it again. One small step for man; one giant leap for mankind. I shouted it out over the whole countryside. Magnificent desolation. Nobody heard.

JODY: *(Taking off helmet.)* Jesus. They're after simulating a bomb. Do you want to look? *(Offers helmet.)*

OLD MAN: I'd as soon not see it.

JODY: Come on. We better get on with this quick. It's looking bad.

(Jody *sets about fixing up the table as a shelter. He begins taking armfuls of books and placing them haphazardly on top of the table. The* OLD MAN *watches him for a while.*)

OLD MAN: What are you doing? I thought Dylan wasn't coming.

JODY: It's for myself. I'm fixing up a place to sleep.

OLD MAN: And what's wrong with this here? *(Indicates lean-to.)*

JODY: Sure aren't you going to be using that?

OLD MAN: And isn't there plenty of room for the two of us?

JODY: You don't think I'm going to spend the night in there with you? Amn't I as well to fix up this while we have time?

OLD MAN: Oh, if that's the way, that's the way. *(Goes to sit down. Picks accordion off chair and looks impatiently for a place to put it. He sits down.* JODY *continues working.)*

OLD MAN: *(Eventually.)* Who is this fella anyway?

JODY: What fella?

OLD MAN: You know well what fella. The fella Pat is shacked up with. The fella that's playing father to you son. Who is he?

JODY: "Who" is he? What do you mean "who" is he? "Who" is anyone? "Who" am I?

OLD MAN: All right so. WHAT is he?

JODY: "What is he?" What does that mean?

OLD MAN: What does he do with himself?

JODY: I dunno. This and that.

OLD MAN: A double jobber! Hah! Begod he sounds a great man altogether, that can hold down two jobs. And you not able to have even one.

JODY: He has no job. Sure who has a job now? What job have you, if it comes to that?

OLD MAN: I'm retired, as you well know. I have discharged my responsibilities to my family and to society.

JODY: Your family.

OLD MAN: Yes. My family. Has this fella any occupation? Any specialisation?

JODY: He writes.

OLD MAN: What does he write?

JODY: Books. I think.

OLD MAN: Just what the world needs. One great book that will lock the savagery out for ever more. Or is it lock it in?

JODY: He's all right. He's doin' his best...It's not his fault things are the way they are.

OLD MAN: Well I don't know whose fault it's supposed to be, but I know that it's no way to bring up a young fella like that — to have a parade of blokes coming in year upon year acting the father and then revvin' up and effin' off.

JODY: It's not like that. It just has to be sorted out. There's no point in making bad blood.

OLD MAN: What d'ya call him anyway, this fella?

JODY: How do you mean, "What do I call him"?

OLD MAN: Does he have a name? Where does he come out of? Who is he?

JODY: Yes. He has a name. Simon.

OLD MAN: Simon. Simon what? Simon Simple...Simple Simon. Who is he?

JODY: Who is he? Who am I? Who the fuck is anybody? His name is Simon Rowntree. And no, he's not one of the Patrick Street Rowntrees, or the Ballinakissmearse Rowntrees or the Cloonacunty Rowntrees. He's a Rowntree. He might be one of the fucken Jupiter Rowntrees for all I know.

OLD MAN: That's a nice way to talk.

JODY: Look. I'm sorry. But that's the way it is. Look, can you not leave it alone. I'm not here with you because I want to be. I mean I am. But I'm not. It's not...It's nothing to do with who I am or who you are or what I do or what I don't do. Or what she is or who he is or what he does. He is. I am. He's there. I'm here. We're all where we are because that's the fucken way it is.

OLD MAN: Oh, lovely!

JODY: There's nothing I can do, or you can do. We just have to let things sort themselves out in their own way and hope for the best. It's not as simple as you're trying to make out. It's not like it was in your day. It's not as easy as it was — if it ever was. Things have changed.

OLD MAN: They have surely. And not for the better either.

JODY: Look at yourself. Look at me. Look at the set-up there was here.

OLD MAN: Why do you always have to draw that down?

JODY: No. No. You don't want to talk about that.

OLD MAN: We've been down that road a thousand times.

JODY: We have. But we're still not too sure where it leads to.

OLD MAN: At least we know where we stand. Which is more than can be said for young Dylan.

(Looks at JODY *carefully building the books on the table.)*

OLD MAN: What d'ya think you're doing now?

JODY: I'm building the books up.

OLD MAN: Buildin' the books up. Did you not read the booklet?

JODY: I did. I read enough of it.

OLD MAN: Well, if you read it you'd know that you're supposed to prop the table up on bricks. Didn't I tell you there was a few out there in the yard. Why do you think I spent an hour washing them this morning?

JODY: Sure isn't the table high enough the way it is?

OLD MAN: More of it.

JODY: We're not having a dance under it.

OLD MAN: More of it.

JODY: What?

OLD MAN: Whether it's high enough or low enough is not the point. The point is that if you put a load of stuff on top of that table you'll drive the four legs through the carpet, and maybe through the floor as well.

JODY: Oh.

OLD MAN: Oh!

JODY: Sorry, I didn't think.

OLD MAN: No, you didn't. You never do.

JODY: Why are you always finding fault?

OLD MAN: I'm only trying to show you the right way of doing things.

JODY: The right way of doing things? You mean your way of doing things.

OLD MAN: There's a right way and a wrong way.

JODY: Or maybe there's twenty right ways and fifty wrong ways. Everything doesn't have to be your way.

OLD MAN: No one ever said it had. There was a time when you used to like me to show you how to do things.

JODY: I did. Twenty years ago, maybe. I did. I'm a grown man now.

OLD MAN: Then it's time you started to act like one.

JODY: And that's what I'm doin'.

OLD MAN: Go on, so. If that's your attitude. Do it your own way.

JODY: I will. I will do it my own way. For once in my life, I'll do it my own way. For once in my life I'll take charge. Anyway, why do I have to be like you?

OLD MAN: It's not a question of being like me. No one ever said you had to be like me. I don't want you to be like me. I want you to be yourself, for Christ's sake.

JODY: All right. I'll go and get some of those bricks.

(JODY *exits.*)

OLD MAN: But you are whether you like it or not. You are whether you see it or not.

(OLD MAN *sweeps up remains of earth from the floor. Suddenly, a burst of music comes from the Virtual Reality helmet. It is Joy Divisions's 'Love Will Tear Us Apart', which the* OLD MAN *remembers from his youth. He begins to groove to the music, using sweeping brush as "guitar", culminating in a pogo jump. He fails to notice that* JODY *has returned and is standing at the door, carrying bricks.* JODY *watches for a moment in puzzlement, then leaves again to avoid embarrassment. In a moment,* JODY *makes a deliberately noisy entrance and the* OLD MAN *hurriedly resumes sweeping.)*

JODY: I thought you said there was half a dozen bricks left out there. I can only find three.

OLD MAN: I must've used the others for the window.

JODY: I'll have to put something else under the table. I know...*(He goes across and picks up Bible.)*...the Bible!

OLD MAN: *(Grabbing it from his hand.)* You're not puttin' the Bible under the leg of the table.

JODY: Why not? It's just about the right size.

OLD MAN: If you think I'm going up to face Saint Peter leaving the Holy Bible under the leg of the table you have another think coming. What about *Ulysses*? *(Holds up book.)*

JODY: Not thick enough.

OLD MAN: *(Picks up another book and tosses it across.)* Here try this.

JODY: What is it?

OLD MAN: *The Satanic Verses.* That should be safe enough.

(The helmet emits a loud bang and a flash.)

OLD MAN: Oh Jesus.

FEMALE PRESENTER: The Ayatollah said that he was putting the world on notice that the word of the prophets could no longer be disregarded. The people of Lot disbelieved our warnings. We let loose on them a stone-charged whirlwind which destroyed them all. Taste my punishment now that you have scorned my warnings... *(The signal breaks up and voice becomes indecipherable. They anxiously shake and bang device in an attempt to get reception back, without success.)*

OLD MAN: Whirlwind. Did you hear that? You should get up there now while you still have the chance.

JODY: I said leave it.

OLD MAN: For Christ's sake, you're the lad's father.

JODY: I'll be his father. Don't you worry.

OLD MAN: Someone has to worry.

JODY: I'll be the kind of father that I want to be.

OLD MAN: There's only one kind of father.

JODY: Ah, how would you know? You never had a son.

OLD MAN: *(Hurt.)* Maybe not. But I brought you up since you were that high. Does that count for nothing?

JODY: *(Taken aback.)* Yes. I know. I'm not saying... You're not my father. I never knew him. But I'm still him. And my son is me.

OLD MAN: Jesus, but you're simple. Do you think having a son is like having a pet dog? *(Mimes calling a dog.)* Here boy. Here boy. *(Whistles.)*

JODY: No. No. But it's not as straightforward as it used to be. A child can have a mother, and he can have a father. They don't have to be a couple. Not anymore. He can live with her and I can have him at the weekends. We can go to football matches...

OLD MAN: You don't like football!

JODY: I do like football. It's alright. Dylan likes it. The point is that there's more freedom now.

OLD MAN: Freedom! The freedom to go to a football match for a while of a Saturday with a young fella that calls another man his daddy? What age are you now? Thirty? Thirty-one?

JODY: See. You don't know. You don't know what age I am.

OLD MAN: Freedom how are ya. The freedom to be left for dead in the gutters of New York.

JODY: You envied him. You told me so yourself.

OLD MAN: I envied him, yes. But I despised him as well.

JODY: Oh that's it. We're back to badmouthing me father.

OLD MAN: I don't want to badmouth him. He was a good man. But like the rest of us, he wasn't perfect. Jack Kenny and America were well met.

JODY: Were you ever there?

OLD MAN: Where?

JODY: America.

OLD MAN: Me? America? How would I be in America? Hadn't I enough to do here? ?

JODY: Did you never go on a visit even?

OLD MAN: No.

JODY: Did you never want to?

OLD MAN: Oh, I wanted to. But you can't always do what you want. I suppose I didn't want to be disappointed.

JODY: Disappointed? How d'ya mean?

OLD MAN: I don't know. I didn't want to find out what the real America was like. I already had one America in my head. America for us was always a sound. A shape. A smell. Mothballs. Bright colours. It was the sound of places. And the sound of the places took on all the other things as well. Philadelphia.

JODY: Philadelphia here I come.

OLD MAN: Phil. A. Delph. IAAA. Our America came in boxes. Not like Mrs Mullarkey's ould boxes that she'd bring out to put your messages in. And the way she would tie it up with twine from the roll on the counter. And wrap the twine in a secret way around her fingers and — phtt! — Just like that. Just like that. No, these were big, American cardboard boxes with strange brand names. Hershey Bars.

(Sound of static noise from headset. JODY is fiddling with it.)

JODY: There's a loose wire in this thing. Have you a box of matches there? (JODY *gets a candle.)*

OLD MAN: What d'ya want matches for?

JODY: A bit of candle grease will hold this wire in place.

OLD MAN: You'll make a mess of it altogether. The latest technology! *(He rattles the box of matches and tosses it across to* JODY.*)* The box from America...Full of the strangest clothes you'd ever seen. Cast-offs. You wouldn't be seen dead! Couldn't. Stripy shirts with big wide collars. Ties as wide as your chest. Blouses like wallpaper. Pink showerproofs. Did you ever see a pink showerproof? You might get a couple of things. A belt maybe. Imitation leather. Or maybe a shirt that if you wore a coat over it to the bog wouldn't look too bad. The rest would go back in the box and straight up into the attic. And the ould fella would sit down and spend a whole Sunday writing a thank-you letter. Thank you for the lovely bellbottoms!

JODY: *(Going to one of the boxes on the floor.)* It's all here.

OLD MAN: What?

JODY: *(Holds up trousers.)* Thank you for the lovely bellbottoms.

OLD MAN: It was there all the time?

JODY: Yeah. On a wet day we used to go up on the attic and spend hours rummaging through all the boxes. Pretending to be Yanks.

OLD MAN: We used to do that too. We used to fantasise about the people who had worn them before. What were they like? There would have been more use made out of a parcel from Mars. Little green aunts! But we knew they were our aunts — and uncles. But mostly aunts. And what did they think we were like? *(They hold up a series of bizarre American-style garments and parade about the place with them. After a few moments there's a knocking at the front door. The OLD MAN grabs a hurley stick from the corner.)*

OLD MAN: Shhh! Shhh. Don't make any sound. Maybe they'll go away.

(The knocking ceases and JODY quietly takes the hurley stick from OLD MAN's hand. JODY picks up another box of books and empties it on to the table. He continues building with the books. The OLD MAN picks up the brush and resumes sweeping the floor. He watches JODY critically.)

OLD MAN: No, no, no. You're doin' that wrong.

JODY: Well what so? How am I supposed to do it?

OLD MAN: Sure you're only throwin' them up on the table.

JODY: What's wrong with them?

OLD MAN: Can you not build them up properly? You never saw a tradesman building a wall like that.

JODY: That's because I'm not a tradesman, it's not a wall, and it's only a temporary job.

OLD MAN: A temporary job!

JODY: Yes. A temporary job for a temporary situation.

OLD MAN: Temporary situation! That's a good one. A temporary job for a temporary situation. Well, it isn't off the wind you took it.

JODY: How d'ya mean?

OLD MAN: Ah, you remind me of my own father every time I see you mullacking around the place. However you got hold of it. My poor mother had her heart broke listening to it all her life. If there was a broken window, it was patched up with a bit of plywood. A temporary job. And you could be sure you'd be looking at it for at least five years — until the plywood fell apart or someone had the gumption to break another pane of glass and it was either fix it or leave the light on all day. I swear to God my mother used to break the glass herself. A temporary job. If I had a pound for every time I heard my father say that. A temporary job. Jesus, a temporary job!. *(He sweeps the books off the table with the brush.* JODY *is surprised and backs away.)* If a job's worth doing, it's worth doing right. That's what you always heard me say. It's as easy do it right as do it wrong. *(He leaves down the brush and comes across and stands over* JODY *who is picking up the books.)* Take your books. Sort them out according to size. Big ones in one pile. Medium in another. Small books to one side. You put your big books down first. Medium books on top. And so on. Then you can build them up into a pyramid, the way they won't fall off in a heap in the middle of the night.

(The OLD MAN *crosses over and sits down in his armchair as the helmet sparks into life.* JODY *goes to it and fiddles around with it until it goes silent.)*

JODY: What was your father like anyway?

OLD MAN: My father was his own man.

JODY: It wasn't off the wind you took it so!

OLD MAN: What's that? Hmmph?

JODY: Oh nothing. Just counting the books. He was a lot older than you, wasn't he?

OLD MAN: He was fifty when I was born. He was like something from another planet.

JODY: I know the feeling.

OLD MAN: What?

JODY: Nothing. You got on all right, did you?

OLD MAN: We got on on the basis that I was afraid of my life of him. A balance of terror, as you might say.

JODY: Yeah, y'see, that's exactly the kind of thing I want Dylan to be free of. I want him to be himself.

OLD MAN: Well, if you don't help him to become himself he will become nothing. A son is formed by his father whether he knows it or not, or whether he likes it or not.

JODY: That's where you're wrong. You didn't become like your father.

OLD MAN: I didn't say become like, I said formed by. The whole way of operating as a man is defined by how you relate to your father.

JODY: That doesn't make it good.

OLD MAN: No. But it makes it happen. That's all. Without it there's nothing. You have to dig deep to bury your father. I am what I am because of what my father was, or seemed to be.

JODY: Did you love him?

OLD MAN: Love? What's love got to do with it? We went through the motions. But to love someone you have to know them first, and no man alive ever knows anything about his father. But that doesn't mean he isn't necessary. I remember as a child doing the Stations of the Cross with my father, night after night. I would wait for him until he finished work and we would walk to the chapel together. If you saw us you would say that we were the two ripest candidates for canonisation you ever saw. Hands joined, heads bowed. But my head was full of every kind of debauchery and blasphemy you could think of. Dirty pictures. And I'm pretty sure his was no different. I'm not just talking pretence — like the Pharisees in the Temple. This wasn't for public consumption. This was just between ourselves, a little charade for our mutual benefit. Neither of us knew any other way of behaving. It's the trap of father and son. Neither can escape it. A man becomes a father and begins to act like he thinks a father should act, so he can pass on to his son a version of living that he himself couldn't live up to. He ends up by trapping them both. But I don't know any other way. Do you?

JODY: Yes. It doesn't have to be like that. You could've been truthful with one another.

OLD MAN: And where would that have got us? D'you think any son wants to find out that his father is human?

(Helmet splutters into life again. JODY begins fiddling with it. It bursts into sound.)

MALE PRESENTER: ...routed and put to flight. The hour of doom is their appointed time, more calamitous, and more doleful, shall that hour be than all their worldly trials.

FEMALE PRESENTER: And right now is our appointed time for the weather forecast...*(Helmet breaks into spluttering again. JODY gives it a slap and it goes off. JODY turns round and looks at OLD MAN, who is now dozing off.)*

JODY: Dad. Are you awake? *(There is no answer. JODY walks around the sleeping figure of the OLD MAN, examining him in minute detail.)*

JODY: What are you like? Where, in the name of Jesus, did they spring you from? Who are you to me? I woke up and found you there. And me? I might be a man from Mars, for all I know. It wouldn't surprise me in the least, to wake up one morning and find that me face had turned green and I'd sprouted two fucken aerials from the top of me head. There you are now, I'd say. *(He picks up more books.)* I must be about my father's business. *(He looks around the room.)* And this here. This is as plausible as anything else. *(Goes to barricaded window but, unable to see out, gestures towards street outside.)* That street out there. Home. That's a good one. In the beginning was the sound of the street. It said something...The. World. Is. Not. Your. Friend. I would lie in bed listening to the sounds at night. The cars growing nearer and nearer... Vrrrrmmmmmmmmmmm. Mmmmmmmmmmmmmmmmmmmmm. Mm-mmmmmmmmmmmmmmm...*(Mimics car noises.)* until you could make out the distinct sounds that gave them away. Every exhaust with a rattle to match the face of its driver. And then in the morning to walk through those streets to eight o'clock Mass. The scent of the new rain on the breeze-dried dust, like the taste of a penny on the tongue. The town I had been told to call home. Not only had the town been here before I was born but the thoughts that made up the lives of the people who had somehow built this street in its particular configuration, with just that colour of concrete, that narrowness of window, that shape of doorway. *(Makes sound of football crowd roar.)* Ahhhhhhhhhhhhhhhhhhhhhhhhhhhhhhhhhhhhhhhhhhhhh. Ah-hhhhhhhhhhhhhhhhhhhhhhrrrrrrgggggggggggggggggggggghhhhh. My tiny hand shelled within yours. Big and bony. Aaaaaa-hhhhhhhhhhhhhhhhhhhhhhhhhhhhhh. "He's at the forty yard line he's at the thirty-five he's at the thirty he swerves he stops he turns he kicks and its...over the bar and its a point a point another point for the Big Man from North Kerry". And you tightening your grip on my hand and sighing softly, "Themselves and their football." Nothing moved except ourselves, as though the sun had put the town to sleep with the wireless on. The smell of dinner and polish that always came from other people's homes. Father and son, for all the world might know. Me taking in this strange man, this figure inside in this long black coat. *(Pauses.)* Or arriving into the bar with its polished wood and the smell of a thousand different drinks. "How's the youngfellah?" "It's great to be young, but the young never get to know that til it's too late." "You cannot tell a young person how short life is." "True for you. True for you. These are the best days of your life, youngfellah, d'ya hear that?" I loved to listen to the way you would talk. This was the only way I ever knew you. It was in these moments I grew to like you, when I could see that others liked you, and to regard me as someone worthwhile on that account. Sometimes, still, we make sense to one another. A little. I dunno. A private joke maybe. I never laugh as truly as at one of those. But then it's gone. And: silence. Well, not silence...talk, noise...It's like we lost our language or something — the language we both understood. Even the things we talk about do not belong to us. They're not our concern, except at some superficial level of our lives. We pluck them from the air like crab apples. More often they fall between us and we say something in surprise. I watch you with your cue cards, writing down every fiddle-fart some gobshite says on...that yoke. Trying to hold on to the world. Trying to TALK TO ME! That fucken man. *(Bangs table with book.)* Jesus!

(OLD MAN *wakes with a thump.*)

OLD MAN: You should have married that other girl you used to hang around with. Deirdre. She was a nice enough girl.

JODY: Well, Jesus, you're good. Jesus, you're the best ever. I shoulda married Deirdre. You spent two solid years tellin' me she was no good. Not suited. Not our type, you said. A nice enough girl, he tells me now. I was the bigger fool to listen to you at all.

OLD MAN: Sure you never did. Amn't I sick and sore tryin' to get you to do the right thing.

JODY: Not good enough...Not our type...Since when are we the one type anyway?

OLD MAN: Oh that's it. Find an excuse. It's all your poor father's fault now.

JODY: Blood is thicker than water.

OLD MAN: Well there's something fecken thick about you. That's for sure. Wherever you got it.

JODY: Well you never left me in any doubt about that, did ya. "A beggar and his accordion left for dead in the gutters of New York" — as you remind me at every possible opportunity.

OLD MAN: I'm reminding you for your own good. You seem hell bent on following his footsteps. You should go up there while you still have time.

JODY: And do what?

OLD MAN: Lay it on the line. Say you want your son down here with you, not up there in the care of some stranger.

JODY: He's not a stranger. Anyway, Pat is well able to look out for him.

(Burst of static emanates from headset. JODY fiddles with it, and then goes to get candle and attempts to re-fix headset during the following.)

FEMALE PRESENTER: But when the supreme disaster strikes — the day when man will call to mind his labours — when the Fire is brought in sight of all — he that transgressed and chose this present life shall have his home in Hell; but he that feared to stand before his Lord and curbed his soul's desire shall have his home in paradise. Responding to the Ayatollah's statement, the Prime Minister said that the Western world would not be intimidated by...*(Signal breaks up into static.)*

OLD MAN: The boy needs a father. Especially at a time like this.

JODY: It's no use. There's no point in talking about it. I can't do anything. It's the way things are.

OLD MAN: The way things are. And how will things ever get any better if we keep giving in to the way things are? And what if we're all to be blown to Kingdom Come?

JODY: Well, if we are we are. If we are it doesn't matter where we are, or who's here. And if we're not, sure we'll be grand and I'll see him in a few days.

FEMALE PRESENTER: We have the power to destroy them and to replace them by others better than them: nothing can hinder us from so doing. So leave them to amuse themselves and blunder about in their folly until they face the day with which they are threatened; the day when they shall rush forward from their graves, like men rallying to a standard, with downcast eyes and countenances distorted with shame. When the earth shakes and quivers, and the mountains crumble away and scatter abroad into fine dust, you shall be divided into three multitudes: Those on the right...

MALE PRESENTER: Blessed be those on the right.

FEMALE PRESENTER: Those on the left.

MALE PRESENTER: Damned shall be those on the left.

FEMALE PRESENTER: And those to the fore.

MALE PRESENTER: Foremost shall be those.

FEMALE PRESENTER: Such are they that shall be brought near to their Lord in the gardens of delight: a whole multitude from the men of old, but only a few from the latter generations. They shall recline on jewelled couches face to face.

(A loud noise grows to a crescendo in the headset, culminating in a loud explosion, smoke and sparks. All lights go out, leaving JODY holding lighted candle.)

OLD MAN: *(Blesses himself.)* Ah, Mother of shite.

JODY: Jesus Christ on a bike. We're fucked. (JODY *blows candle out.*)

BLACKOUT.

END OF ACT ONE.

ACT TWO

The preparation of the room has been completed. Some time has passed, possibly several weeks. The room is quiet. The electricity has remained off. The room is lit with candles. The headset is connected to a portable power supply, but is not functioning correctly — all that can be heard is a hiss of static. The shelter which JODY was constructing with books in Act One has been completed. It resembles a miniature church, comprising a pyramid of books built around the table, with an opening at the front through which Jody can enter and leave.

The OLD MAN *sits in armchair reading a copy of* **Ulysses**. JODY *crawls around insect-like, wearing the helmet, attempting to find the best spot for reception. All that can be heard is a fluctuating hiss of static.* JODY *inadvertently bumps into* OLD MAN's *legs, and removes helmet.* OLD MAN *scowls and continues reading.* JODY *stands up and examines helmet.* OLD MAN *finishes his book.)*

OLD MAN: "and yes I said yes I will yes". Well thanks be to Jesus I finished that. *(He gets up and begins walking briskly back and forth across the floor, exercising.)*

JODY: What time is it?

OLD MAN: I don't know. The clock's stopped.

JODY: What day is it?

OLD MAN: Tuesday. Or Wednesday. I think. I've lost count. Does it matter?

JODY: We're going to have to start thinking of going out.

OLD MAN: It's not safe.

JODY: How do you know it's not safe.

OLD MAN: It's not safe until someone tells us it is.

JODY: Who's going to tell us? And how...pray...are they going to tell us? Are they going to send us a telegram?

OLD MAN: Be as sarcastic as you like. It doesn't matter. If you open that door as much as one inch, we could be fried where we stand. Anyway, what loss is on us? Haven't we enough to eat?

JODY: We haven't.

OLD MAN: Hah?

JODY: We had the last tin of beans for breakfast.

OLD MAN: Well, I'd rather starve than burn any day.

JODY: You might not have a choice about it.

OLD MAN: *(Goes to barricaded window, listening.)* Can you hear anything out there?

JODY: How would you hear anything? Haven't you everything barricaded up?

OLD MAN: We may as well have a tin of potatoes.

JODY: *(Takes tin from box and opens it.)* These don't look too good to me.

OLD MAN: What's wrong with them?

JODY: I dunno. They're all blotchy and brown-looking.

OLD MAN: Let me see. Christ, the smell of those. Where in the name of God did you get them?

JODY: In the supermarket.

OLD MAN: Ah Jesus, would you look at the sell-by date. They must have them since the 1900s. They saw you comin', hah?

JODY: That fat fucker. I'll have him closed down.

OLD MAN: Is there any more?

JODY: *(Taking out another tin.)* The last one. *(He places it on the middle of the floor and opens it ritualistically. Kneeling on either side, they stretch forward to sniff the tin. Both recoil simultaneously.)*

OLD MAN: Phew!

JODY: Jesus! These are worse.

OLD MAN: Maybe they're not as bad as they smell.

JODY: Jesus, I'm hungry, but I'm not that hungry. Yet.

OLD MAN: Well, any suggestions?

JODY: I suppose we'll have to wait until the phone comes back or the power is restored or something.

OLD MAN: Very helpful, I'm sure.

JODY: Well, what do you propose?

OLD MAN: I don't know.

JODY: That's something anyway.

OLD MAN: What?

JODY: That's a first. John Forde doesn't know!

OLD MAN: You're fierce smart, right enough. We could be the last two men on the planet for all you know. Men. Of mice and men. Bloody scarecrow!

JODY: I did me best.

OLD MAN: Your best.

JODY: Who are you? Huh? You can pontificate all you like. All your ould guff. But it's no use. Blood is thicker than water.

OLD MAN: Is that right? And how much blood would you reckon it'd take to better the Atlantic ocean? Yes, blood is thicker than water.

(JODY, *responding to the implicit jibe, picks up a hand-cranked gramophone/record player, places it on the roof of the "church" and goes to boxes, rummaging. He produces a record and holds it up.* OLD MAN *has been observing him.* JODY *puts record on turntable, cranks up and places needle on record. The voice of Jack Kenny can be heard:*)

VOICE: Howya John. This is your old friend Jack Kenny. I'm here in the Big Apple and everything's grand. How is Margaret and young Jody. Hope ye're well. Here's an ould tune you might like. *(He plays 'The Dawning of the Day' on his accordion. After a couple of bars, the* OLD MAN *rises and rushes to remove record.)*

38

JODY: I have to find my own way. It's like you're always trying to...compensate or something. I don't know.

OLD MAN: Compensate? I have no call to compensate. I did what was right. Always. Not once did I sell you short. Not once in your life. I did what had to be done. Always.

JODY: But that's it. You don't understand. You're on the outside. looking in. You can't see straight. You push too hard.

OLD MAN: How d'you mean "push too hard"? I never pushed you...

JODY: No? What about John Flanagan?

OLD MAN: What about him? What's he got to do with it?

JODY: A good question. John Flanagan, the boy who had everything. John Flanagan, the boy who got honours in every exam he ever sat. John Flanagan, superman. The last we heard of him he was languishing in Mountjoy Prison on 65 counts of fraud and extortion.

OLD MAN: You can twist things as much as you like. That poor fella drove himself too hard. He was a grand young fella when I knew him.

JODY: Yeah? And what about me? Was I not a grand young fella? Could I do anything right? Does the fact that I have, thus far in my existence, refrained from ripping off pension funds, does that not count for anything in your scheme of things?

OLD MAN: John Flanagan is neither here not there. You're my son. I wanted you to do well.

JODY: There you go again. I'm not your son, any more than John Flanagan was.

OLD MAN: What are you trying to tell me? That this is all my fault?

JODY: Yes.

OLD MAN: Jesus.

JODY: The world is different now.

OLD MAN: You can say that again.

JODY: He who must be obeyed. Because of the way you and your like carried on, we have to walk on eggshells.

OLD MAN: No. It's that you don't know how to handle women. That's all. You never did. You don't understand them.

JODY: And you do?

OLD MAN: When you can hold a marriage down for ten years you can begin to talk. Margaret and I were very happy.

JODY: Were you now?

OLD MAN: What do you mean?

JODY: I mean, d'ya know what it was like to be in the house when you were there? Did you have any idea the...the...the pall you brought down upon the place when you walked in the door. The darkness. Like clouds gathering. I could feel it in myself, in her, and in the very light of the room. The greyness, the foreboding, the fear.

OLD MAN: What d'ya mean "fear". She never had cause to be afraid of me. And neither had you. I never raised a hand to either of you.

JODY: No. You didn't have to. You brought us to heel with the furrow of your brow. We spent our days on tenterhooks, watching your every grimace, waiting for the flicker of a smile. She was bowed down with the shadow you cast on her, with your long black coat and your longer, blacker face. I could feel the way she moved with a lighter step once she heard the door close behind you. She would dance and smile like she never did when you were there.

OLD MAN: You always took her side.

JODY: Yes. Yes. Yes. Because you decided that there were two sides to be taken. So I took her side. Yes. D'ya remember that day you drove us out the country.

OLD MAN: Ah sure we drove out the country hundreds of times.

JODY: When we came back you had to go to work in the office.

OLD MAN: I don't remember that.

JODY: She said she'd go home to get the tea ready. And I looked at you and your face said, "Wait." So I sat there and waited. But in a few minutes I got this feeling that I should go after her. And I ran down the street. But then I thought I should tell you where I was going. So I ran back. But halfway back, I thought "I'm going to miss her." So I turned again and ran back towards the house.

OLD MAN: Well, it was a nice howdyado for me to come out and find you gone.

JODY: But you don't remember?

OLD MAN: No. I don't remember.

JODY: And I knocked and knocked on the door, crying out: "I'm here, I'm here. Mammy. I'm here." And in a few minutes she came out of Flanagan's and smiled at me. You don't remember?

OLD MAN: I don't remember.

JODY: And a week later she was dead.

OLD MAN: What are you sayin'? What's that to do with it?

JODY: I'm sayin'...I dunno...I'm saying I couldn't tell her.

OLD MAN: Tell her what?

JODY: I can remember her funeral. I remember her lying in the bed with her toes stuck in the air, making a tent of the bedclothes. And I remember the rain. You sent me across the road to stay with Flanagans. They put me to bed. I was crying. "What are you crying for?" Mrs. Flanagan asked me. "Did you hurt yourself?" I was only — what? — eight? Nine? It didn't seem to occur to her that what had happened would mean anything to me. "Mammy's dead," I said. "There, there," she said. "She's gone to be with the angels. You'll be all right in the morning." I stood inside the window looking out. I saw the hearse pull up in the rain. Pelting down, it was. All day and all night. I saw them take the coffin in. I could see the drops of water on it — glittering. It seemed strange to see this box going in our front door. I watched the light in the window like the light of another planet. Then they brought the coffin out. You were helping to carry it. There was a crowd of people gathered around in the rain. Then they scattered to the cars and the funeral pulled away. There was nobody left except me.

OLD MAN: You were only a boy. You shouldn't blame yourself...

JODY: I'm not. I'm blaming you. You and your...solemnity. You and your gravity. I...I...loved her as my mother.

OLD MAN: Yes, yes.

JODY: But I never told her. Because I didn't know how. You never showed me. I didn't have the words, because you never told me what they were.

OLD MAN: Words. Words. Words. What use are words? It's what you do that counts. You have to do your duty. Be practical. Face up to your responsibilities. We did the right thing by you.

JODY: That's what they all say. "You won't find a soul in this town will say a bad word about John Forde." That man, they tell me, is a saint. That's what they tell me.

OLD MAN: Who? I never claimed to be a saint. I only ever tried to be a proper father.

JODY: And what about a proper husband?

OLD MAN: That too. It goes without saying.

JODY: But you cannot be both.

OLD MAN: Who says?

JODY: I say. You can't be your kind of father and any kind of husband.

OLD MAN: So that's your theory is it?

JODY: It's not a matter of theory. It's a matter of fact.

(A sudden noise is heard. A dead bird, some twigs and soot come down the chimney.)

JODY: Jesus Christ tonight.

OLD MAN: What is it?

JODY: Jesus, it's some class of a bird. A crow. He's after coming down the chimney.

OLD MAN: Is he dead or alive?

JODY: *(Holding up bird for inspection.)* Dead. By the looks of him.

OLD MAN: That's not a crow.

JODY: It is a crow so.

OLD MAN: It's not a crow. It's a rook.

JODY: Well, crows we always called them fellas.

OLD MAN: Well, that's where you're wrong. Rooks are members of the crow family....

JODY: It's a crow.

OLD MAN: And if a fecken tiger came down that chimney, you'd say it was a cat. Your tiger may be a member of the cat family, but would you pet one?

JODY: *(Examining bird.)* I wonder what he tastes like?

OLD MAN: What?

JODY: Boris.

OLD MAN: Who?

JODY: Boris the crow. Rook. I wonder what he tastes like?

OLD MAN: What? Are you off your head?

JODY: Why not?

OLD MAN: What d'ya think he died of?

JODY: I dunno. Maybe he had an accident.

OLD MAN: An accident.

JODY: Yeah. You know. A mid-air collision.

OLD MAN: Yeah. Maybe with a Scud.

JODY: What the fuck is a Scud?

OLD MAN: Ahh! But what if he died of radiation poisoning? Where's that booklet?

JODY: He looks all right to me. It's better than starvin' to death.

(OLD MAN *finds booklet and reads.*)

OLD MAN: "If the animal is tired and lies down a lot...Or if you notice the animal's appetite decreasing..." Ah, that's no help.

JODY: *(Holding up the expired "crow".)* I'd be inclined to chance it anyway.

OLD MAN: Look, if you eat that thing and he died of radiation poisoning, you're a gonner yourself.

JODY: Yeah, but if he didn't...

OLD MAN: Well if he didn't, you can walk out that door. It's perfectly safe. If he did, you can't eat him. If he didn't, there's no need to. *(Sarcastically.)* "If we are we are, and it doesn't matter who's here. And if we're not, sure it'll be grand, and I'll see him in a couple of days."

JODY: Jesus, maybe outside is better than in here. I think I'll chance the door.

OLD MAN: *(Shouts)* Don't go near that bloody door!

(JODY stops and they face off each other. OLD MAN sits in his armchair. Jody places the dead crow on top of the book shelter. He goes and picks up accordion and in a mocking manner plays the Dead March over the crow. He looks over and meets the OLD MAN's disapproving glare. He stops.)

OLD MAN: Jesus, that's all we need.

(JODY sits down on floor in front of book shelter and absent-mindedly doodles on the accordion. OLD MAN rises and menacingly crosses to tower above JODY, who sheepishly stops playing.)

OLD MAN: I never liked that squawkbox. If there's music in Hell it'll be played on the accordion.

JODY: Ah sure, it's in the blood.

OLD MAN: What's this they used to say was a gentleman? Hmmph? A gentleman is someone who can play the accordion, but doesn't.

JODY: And what does that say about my father?

OLD MAN: Your father. Your father. Ah, what d'you know about him?

JODY: Mrs Flanagan told me all about him. When he was...I dunno...I suppose about my age now. No, younger. A bit. She told me about how he stayed in the house next door, in digs. Conways?

OLD MAN: And...?

JODY: He was handsome, she said. He used to read a lot. Brains to burn, she said. Your father. *(Mimics.)* "Morning till night with his nose stuck in some book". He used to stand for hours on the bottom step of the stairs — reading.

OLD MAN: That was me.

JODY: What?

OLD MAN: That was me. Musicians don't read books. It was me standing on the bottom step of the stairs. It was the only decent bulb in the house. The most Jack Kenny ever read was the racing page in the evening paper.

JODY: Oh, here we go again. A loser! A waster!

OLD MAN: He couldn't seem to come to terms with the world at all. He couldn't organise a sandwich in Kinnegad. But I'll tell you something else: unlike you, he was no quitter.

JODY: No quitter?

OLD MAN: No...

JODY: Is this a new slant on things now? What happened to the unfortunate Jack Kenny? The loser, the ne'er-do-well.

OLD MAN: I never said anything like that about Jack Kenny.

JODY: The waster.

OLD MAN: It was you I was talking about.

JODY: That's all you ever had to say about either of us. "Like father, like son."

OLD MAN: Well, he was no coward. You can be sure he went down fightin'.

JODY: Oh yeah. If you thought he was in bad shape you should have seen the state of the bus!

OLD MAN: What bus? What are you talkin' about?

JODY: Sure we might as well make it a bus while we're at it.

OLD MAN: What?

JODY: The hit-and-run. Or maybe a train?

OLD MAN: Oh do, make a skit of it. The poor ould divil. *(Pause)* Look, there was no hit and run. The facts are...

JODY: Facts? That'd be a change!

OLD MAN: Yes...The facts are that he was killed in a street fight, and left for dead in the gutters of New York with his head split open. But you can be sure he took a couple of them with him.

JODY: A hit-and-run. That's what you told me yourself.

OLD MAN: That was a story cobbled together by the women to stop the tongues wagging around this arsehole of a town.

(JODY *goes and picks up an old wooden box filled with personal papers. He searches through them.*)

JODY: I remember it like it was five minutes ago. I remember you calling to the school and taking me to the church. There was a memorial service, but no coffin. I remember the smell of incense in the church from a previous funeral. The music. 'Jesus, Joy of Man's Desiring.' That was the first time I heard of Jack Kenny. Killed in New York by a hit-and-run driver, you said. "Who was Jack Kenny," I asked. "Jack Kenny was your father," you said. "No," I said, "You're me father." You just shook your head.

(OLD MAN *remains silent.*)

JODY: Six years old and suddenly I had a new father who no longer existed.

OLD MAN: There were reasons for telling you. It suited.

JODY: Suited? What d'ya mean "suited"?

OLD MAN: That was a story, to make it more...respectable.

JODY: No. That's not right. No. Wait a minute.

(Finds letter amongst personal papers in box. He takes letter from envelope and triumphantly presents it under OLD MAN'*s nose. The* OLD MAN, *recognising letter, turns away.)*

JODY: See. That's not the way it happened. See. *(He skip-reads through the letter, picking out relevant phrases.)* "He was found in the snow, could've been a hit and run driver." See. I told you.

(The OLD MAN *remembers the letter in detail without looking at it.)*

JODY: "It was away down town where there isn't much traffic...(*Mumbles through section of letter.)* Lord have mercy on him. Love to all, from Aunt Sheila." See? A hit-and-run driver. See? That's what it says.

OLD MAN: Four pages of a letter. And the first three pages full of...soft chat. "How are all the neighbours." Look at the writing. Big — all spaced out, like she's trying to cover as much space as possible. Turn to the last bit. It nearly didn't fit. The bit about Jack. Look. The writing gets smaller and smaller as you get to the end of the page.

JODY: So?

OLD MAN: So it's clear from the way she's hunker-sliding around the place that something isn't right. D'ya not see through it? It's because she knows the truth. And she knows I suspect the truth. But she also knows that there is a need to avoid the truth in the interest of...decency.

JODY: So what you're telling me now is this was all lies.

OLD MAN: No. Not lies. Economies.

JODY: But why?

OLD MAN: Out of wanting to do what was right. Wanting to construct a version of events that everyone could live with.

JODY: That who could live with? You? Aunt Sheila? Who?

OLD MAN: You, Jody. It was done for you. That was the way things were handled. People had consideration. Feelings. There was no need for the truth to come out.

JODY: And now? Now it's all right?

OLD MAN: No. But if it stops you believing that this yellow streak in you is inherited from your father...

JODY: You're just twistin' the truth to suit yourself.

OLD MAN: Your weakness. Your spinelessness. You and your fear. That's what has brought us to this. You here and your son a hundred miles away. Dead or alive? We don't know.

JODY: Alive. Alive. Anyway, what's it to you? He's my son.

OLD MAN: And I'm his...I'm your father.

JODY: No you're not. You're my guardian. That's it. To Dylan, you're nothing.

OLD MAN: I'm nothing! Is that it?

JODY: All right, you're not me real father, is what I'm saying. And Dylan — of course he sees you as his grandfather. There's no question about that. For him there's no difference.

OLD MAN: How d'you mean, "no difference". Of course there's a difference.

JODY: He loves you as his grandad. What's "grandad" anyway? It's just a word. What's "father"? A word.

OLD MAN: A word!?

JODY: Yes, a word. It's the same for Dylan as it was for me.

OLD MAN: I see.

JODY: That's how I grew up. It didn't kill me.

OLD MAN: So, you're saying what? That "I've had my son and now I've lost him. So be it."

JODY: No. I'm saying the world has changed.

OLD MAN: Mea culpa, mea culpa, mea maxima culpa.

JODY: As you keep telling me yourself, it's a question of practicalities. The function of the male has changed. Anyone can perform the role of father.

OLD MAN: Hah!

JODY: Men were in the driving seat for too long. They abused their positions of power and authority. But the worm turned. And now it's payday.

OLD MAN: So because of what some men did — who? — because of that, a man has no rights anymore. The male has nothing to contribute except spunk and spondulicks?

JODY: If you want to put it like that.

OLD MAN: The beasts of the earth.

JODY: Yeah. But the blame is at our own door.

OLD MAN: And what about the family line? What about the family name?

JODY: Ah, what about it?

OLD MAN: I can remember my own grandfather. My father's father. And my father. And me. *(Pause, looks to* JODY.*)* And me. And you. And Dylan.

JODY: It's finished. You see. You can't have it both ways. It's over. Your line is broken. I'm not your son. You have no son.

OLD MAN: No.

JODY: It ends with you.

OLD MAN: No...No...You can't see. It's not just the blood. No...

JODY: I have nothing to hand on either. My line is broken. It bled all over a street in New York. Like you say.

OLD MAN: No. No. You can't see...It's not just the blood...

JODY: Oh! The Gene Genie's back in his box.

OLD MAN: What? Christ! D'ya think I would allow it to end with me?

JODY: What d'ya mean?

OLD MAN: D'ya know anything about me?

JODY: What are you saying?

OLD MAN: Surely you have some clue.

JODY: I don't know what you're on about.

OLD MAN: I didn't think it would ever come to this...

JODY: Well, there you are. Don't blame me — I didn't end it.

OLD MAN: *(Pause.)* I'm your father.

JODY: Ah for Jazus sake.

OLD MAN: No. Listen. I am your father. In every sense of the word.

JODY: Bollix.

OLD MAN: I'm your father.

JODY: What are you saying?

OLD MAN: You heard me. Yes, yes, yes. It's time it was said. It's gone on too long. I'm sorry. It's the truth.

(OLD MAN *sits down in armchair, and after a pause begins to speak in a low voice.*) She was fair. Your mother. Deborah. She was a beauty. She was down from up North. Visiting a friend in town. We used to see her in the street. Me and Jack. Then one night she was there at the pictures in the Savoy. Jack and I always went to the pictures on a Monday. To get out of the digs. She was in the seat behind. The picture was 'Wuthering Heights'. "Who's that?" I asked Jack. He didn't know. She had long blonde hair, the softest, fairest complexion you'd ever seen. She was fragile. On the way out of the cinema, I caught her eye and she smiled. We got talking going down the street. I asked her into the Roma Cafe for a cup of tea. Deborah. There's something about a town late in the evening — maybe half-ten, eleven. A summer evening. The light. The dryness of the street. The smells that hang in the air. It's like it's...liberated...D'ya know?...from all the spite and tightness. Even the meanest, tightest town in creation comes to life at a certain hour of the night if you're with someone you can...dream about. The streetlights on the river, the growl of cars, the hum from a pub door as you pass by. The waft of beer and blasphemy. A moment of togetherness. Real. All the streets dissolved into one. Alive. You feel you can walk about the place without it belonging to anyone other than you. And her. *(Pause)* My father would never wear her. She wasn't our "type". He was the product of a generation that knew the meaning of want. In a country kicked senseless and half-starved to death, there was nothing left to people but a certain idea of what made them good, what made them superior. That meant everything to people like my father. Who you were and who your people were. Not what they had, because very few had anything worth talking about. You created an image of yourself and where you came from. You expressed it in your bearing, the way you walked, the kind of things you said. A kind of nobility. I used to watch him walk about town in his long black coat. Not like he owned the place, but like the place wasn't worth owning.

You were right when you said that I knew nothing about women. I don't understand them. Nothing is what it seems, I often think. So, yes. I had made a commitment to Margaret and we got married. We went away on honeymoon. When I got back I found out that Deborah had taken up with Jack Kenny. The next thing I heard they were getting married. He kept out of my way. Then we had a set-to one night down the town. We had a couple of pints. He told me she was pregnant. He was going to marry her. I took a swing at him. He landed a couple of punches. We were thrown out of the pub and had to be pulled apart out in the street. I was confused. But I didn't know. It never crossed my mind, I swear, that the child might be mine. She was at home all this time, while she was expecting. He was prepared to go through with a marriage and carry on as though the child was his. It was the best way, he said. But she was unsure. He went a few times to try to talk her round, but in the end she wouldn't even see him. I went to see what could be done. I thought that maybe I could talk her into reconciling with Jack, making the best of things, but she wasn't there. She'd taken off after the birth leaving the child with her parents. Her mother told me that she was planning to go to America. I made a deal with Jack. I said we had to take control of the situation. If he helped me get my child back, I would pay his way to America, to start a new life. The baby — you — you were up North a hundred miles away. Margaret and I talked about it and we arranged for Jack to come and live with us as if we were helping him to bring the baby up.

JODY: You didn't tell Mammy that you...

OLD MAN: No. But she knew. Margaret was delighted to have a baby in the house. We didn't know then that she couldn't have any of her own. The whole thing was a blessing in some ways.

JODY: And everyone believed I was his son.

OLD MAN: Yes. Jack used to walk you up the town in your pram. No one doubted it.

JODY: Jesus!

OLD MAN: It's shocking, I know, but when I heard he was dead, all I felt at first was relief. Then guilt. Then sorrow. Now I look back on him and wonder if he ever lived at all.

JODY: You didn't have to do this.

OLD MAN: What?

JODY: You didn't have to construct these elaborate lies. These myths.

OLD MAN: And what?

JODY: And you could have told the truth.

OLD MAN: The truth? How? When? Where would you have me draw the line?

JODY: Line? How d'ya mean draw the line?

OLD MAN: Between the past and reality? Between living and the truth? Where?

JODY: You could've been honest. We're all adults.

OLD MAN: Now. Yes. We're all adults. But not then. You were a boy. You can't tell a child everything. How could they deal with a story so different from what they saw all around? It has to be simple. Mammy. Daddy. Simple.

JODY: Simple! Mammy. Daddy. Simple.

OLD MAN: Yes.

JODY: All that deceit.

OLD MAN: A necessary evil.

JODY: All my life I never had a full father. From that moment in the church...you took my father away.

OLD MAN: The motive was a good one. It's substance that counts, not facts. It's creating something to believe in. Our memories are far more important than what actually happened.

JODY: But don't you see? I did have something to believe in. All you had to do was confirm what I already felt.

OLD MAN: The past is only important to make the present function. Truth is a luxury — for women and priests.

JODY: The lie broke out all over. The respectable option. Social pressures. The town. Fuck the town. You going around the place like the Ayafuckingtollah Almighty with your long black coat and the weight of the world on your shoulders. What's right must also be the truth. Otherwise we rot from the ground up. How can we ever hope to love?

OLD MAN: Love. It's easy for women to talk about love. They're there, you see, from the off. The child comes out, and who does he see? His mother. The father comes in afterwards and has to explain what it is he does.

JODY: And you know the worst of it? For me anyway? You made me like you. You made me in your own image.

OLD MAN: Don't you ever forget, Joseph, that for all their talk about love, women are on the lookout for one thing: a father to replace the one who's going to die soon. And they find him too, no matter what. They cannot fight it. Their fathers are inside them, just like our fathers are inside us. What's a marriage but the smouldering souls of two ould fellas battling for the upper hand?

JODY: It's wrong. It's all wrong.

OLD MAN: It's necessary wrong. Yes, it's necessary evil. But what's the alternative. Hmmph? The alternative is nothing. Nothingness and nothing. Emptiness and death.

JODY: But it was all for nothing. You drove one woman into an early grave, and you turned your back on another woman. My mother.

OLD MAN: A father can't tell the full truth. It's not his to tell. He has to do what's best. What's right. He cannot give in to his own feelings. The weak die. It's like yer man Boris there. How did he die? Maybe he was pecked to death. They do that sometimes. Their instinct tells them they must find the twigs for their own nests. Where d'ya think is the easiest place to find them?

JODY: Ah, I dunno...

OLD MAN: In some other fecken rook's nest. That's where. Rob Peter. But the system doesn't allow that. They daren't steal from each other. If they do, the entire flock descends on the culprit and pecks him to death.

JODY: Maybe they just don't like dishonesty.

OLD MAN: No. No. Emotions don't come into it. It's a question of what works. Morals are just a system of rules backed up by sanctions. But you have to have it, or the whole thing falls apart. Feelings, conscience, guilt, love. They're just devices. I didn't wear a fucking black coat because I liked wearing black coats. I wore it because somebody had to. To keep it going. We can't escape from that. We can't escape from one another. The only freedom we have is the freedom to belong. The freedom to continue. Not to stop — that's what freedom is.

(JODY *claps his hands, once, twice, three times. Then claps aggressively under the* OLD MAN's *nose. Claps are almost like attempts to strike* OLD MAN.)

JODY: Freedom. *(Claps.)* Practical. *(Claps.)* Simple. *(Claps.)* That's simple. *(Claps.)* That's practical. *(Claps again.* OLD MAN *retreats.)* You denied me.

OLD MAN: What? What are you goin' on about?

JODY: You denied me.

OLD MAN: No, I'd never did that.

JODY: At the Feis. The judging was by the amount of clapping.

OLD MAN: What?

JODY: The loudest clap won. You didn't clap me.

OLD MAN: What?

JODY: I watched you. You were talking to a woman beside you. You never clapped. I came second.

OLD MAN: No. No.

JODY: John Flanagan came first. You clapped John Flanagan. And when he won you clapped him again.

OLD MAN: Ah look. I don't know what you're talking about. I can't remember. Clap. Clap. It was only an ould feis.

JODY: See? That's it. That's exactly it. "It was only an ould feis!" It didn't matter to you. But I remember. It mattered to me. I cried a full day after that. You denied me. And why? Because you weren't a complete father? That's what I thought then, and I was right. I thought, he isn't my real father. He doesn't love me.

(OLD MAN *is totally silenced and is unable to meet* JODY's *eyes.* JODY *reads his looking away as confirmation and he breaks downstage to his shelter. He gets into his shelter and the* OLD MAN *approaches as though to appeal to him.* JODY *pulls accordion into the shelter and begins to play in a mindless random fashion.* OLD MAN *retreats and climbs into his own shelter.* JODY *continues "playing" for a few moments. He then stops and a silence ensues. The silence hangs until broken by a cough from the* OLD MAN.)

OLD MAN: Who was that woman I was talking to?

JODY: I don't know. I don't remember.

OLD MAN: Hah. See? It's easy to forget. It was Mrs Cassidy, wasn't it?

JODY: I don't remember.

OLD MAN: Yes, it was Mrs Cassidy. And d'ya know what she said? When you were playin'? She said, "That young fella is the image of his father, with his little accordion." That's why I didn't clap. She knew what she was sayin' too, the ould hairpin. It got to me. I didn't want to be reminded. Not then.

(A long pause, almost an eternity, follows. Eventually JODY emerges from his shelter with a bottle of wine and a biscuit tin. He places them centre stage and kneels beside them.)

JODY: Are you hungry?

OLD MAN: *(After a pause.)* Did you say something?

JODY: I said, are you hungry.

OLD MAN: If I am itself, what's the point in thinking about it?

JODY: I kept something.

OLD MAN: What?

JODY: I kept something for when everything ran out.

(The OLD MAN emerges from his shelter and crawls to JODY.)

OLD MAN: What have you there? Wine? Where did you spring that from?

JODY: A little something for the rainy day.

OLD MAN: 'Tis far from it we were reared. What else have you there?

(JODY opens the tin, which contains Lincoln Cream biscuits. He offers one to the OLD MAN.)

OLD MAN: Lincoln Creams. I like a Lincoln Cream.

JODY: *(He takes a bite.)* Did you ever wonder why they're called Lincoln Creams?

OLD MAN: Why?

JODY: There's no cream in them. Custard Creams have cream in them. But Lincoln Creams have none.

OLD MAN: D'ya remember what we used to call them.

JODY: I do.

OLD MAN: *(Taking a bite from a biscuit.)* Lumpies.

JODY: It's a better name than Lincoln Creams. D'ya remember how you used to bring me up a mug of tea in the morning before you went to work?

OLD MAN: Hmmh?

JODY: And a big fistful of Lumpies. I could smell the tea and you coming up the stairs. Strong and hot and sweet. I used to pretend to be asleep and you used to pretend to wake me up. *(Pause.)* I remember one time when I was sick. I had the measles.

OLD MAN: You almost died that time. Did you know that?

JODY: Yes. I know. I remember you sitting by my bed. You were holding my hand. Time stood still. I remember opening my eyes and seeing the clock.

OLD MAN: And what did it say.

JODY: It said a quarter past.

OLD MAN: A quarter past what?

JODY: Just a quarter past. I opened my eyes, again and again. Each time it was a quarter past. It was like the same moment was lasting forever — like I was suspended over a cliff, waiting to drop. And you sat there holding my hand, whispering to me in the dark. And then I noticed the light creeping through the chink in the curtains. It was a quarter past six. And you stood up and wiped my forehead and let go my hand. And in a few minutes I could smell you coming up the stair with a mug of tea and a fistful of lumpies. I can still smell it.

(A long pause follows, during which they eat their biscuits and drink their wine. Suddenly there is a loud banging at the front door. OLD MAN shushes JODY.)

OLD MAN: Shhh!

JODY: But...

OLD MAN: Shhhh!

(More hammering at door).

JODY: It might...

OLD MAN: Shhh. They'll go away.

JODY: But it might... We could...

OLD MAN: Can't you be quiet?

(More insistent hammering.)

JODY: They might know. We could find out. We could ask. *(He gets up and goes to the door. He can be heard in the hallway.)* Yes. Hello.

(More hammering.)

JODY: Yes. Who is it?

VOICE OUTSIDE: Hellu.

JODY: Yes, hello. Who is it? What do you want?

VOICE: Hellu. Can you open up. *(More hammering.)*

JODY: What do you want?

VOICE: Is that Jim? Hellu, Jim? Can you open up?

OLD MAN: Ask them is it safe? Is it safe?

JODY: What d'ya want? What's happening?

VOICE: Hellu. Hellu. *(More hammering.)*

OLD MAN: Is it safe? Don't open that door unless it's safe.

VOICE: Hellu. Hellu. *(More hammering.)*

JODY: Okay. Okay. Okay. Hang on. *(We hear the noise of objects being removed from the barricaded front door. OLD MAN hides at the side of the wardrobe.)*

JODY: Alright, alright, alright. Hold your horses. *(Eventually he opens the door. Mumbled talking can be heard in hallway, through the room door, which is slightly ajar. Eventually, the VISITOR enters the room. He is a youngish-to-middle-aged man, dressed in a white trench-coat and wearing a sporting-coloured cap and scarf. He is carrying a large bag of chips in one hand. Seeing the bottle* *of wine on the floor he quickly looks around and thinking he is alone he goes for the wine. JODY re-enters. Caught in the act, VISITOR jumps back.)*

VISITOR: How'ya doin'. That's a wet one. Well, any crack? Is Jim about the place? I was looking for Jim. (OLD MAN *appears and the* VISITOR *is surprised. The* VISITOR *moves as if to shake hands with the* OLD MAN *who moves sharply away fearing contamination.)* Ah, good evening, sir. How'ya doin'?

(No response.)

VISITOR: That's a wet one all right. Cold too. Brass monkeys. But sure, once you keep on the move. Sez you. *(He looks around the room.)* What in the name of God..? *(He goes to examine the* OLD MAN's *shelter.)*

OLD MAN: *(To* JODY, *as though* VISITOR *cannot hear.)* Do you think is he safe?

JODY: No loss on him from where I'm standing.

OLD MAN: Is he contaminated? Are there any marks?

JODY: *(Looking closely at* VISITOR.) I can't see anything.

OLD MAN: Any burns? Any bleeding? Any sores? Any raw flesh?

(JODY creeps over to examine VISITOR *who suddenly turns.* JODY *steps back sharply.)*

OLD MAN: And yourself. Any dizzy spells?

VISITOR: Wha?

OLD MAN: Any vomiting?

VISITOR: Not yet anyways. Sez you.

OLD MAN: Diarrhoea?

VISITOR: Not today, sez you. Is it movin' house ye are?

OLD MAN: Hmmph. Where are you after being?

VISITOR: Wha?

OLD MAN: Where are you after coming out of now?

VISITOR: I'm goin' to the match. Are yese not watchin' it? *(He looks around again.)* Have ye no light or what? Here, have a chip, young fella. (JODY *declines silently.*) Is it redecoratin' ye are or what?

OLD MAN: Where are you after coming out of?

VISITOR: Oh, up above. The Big Smoke. We're headin' down for the match.

OLD MAN: Where were you the last week? While all the fuss was on?

VISITOR: *(Scratches head.)* Now there you have me. That's a tough wan, sez you. Where was I? Rumour has it I was in intensive care. Ha, ha, ha! Sez you, can I get back to you on that? No! I know. Sez you. I was in Baghdad. Did you ever hear that wan? I was in Baghdad when you were in dad's bag. Hah. Isn't it a good wan? *(He suddenly notices the Virtual Reality helmet.)* Jasus I haven't seen one of those yokes in years. *(He goes over and picks it up and starts to try it out.)*

OLD MAN: Jesus, is there any sense to be got out of the fella at all? *(Then loudly.)* Were you not indoors?

VISITOR: Hah?

OLD MAN: The alert. Were you not in shelter?

VISITOR: Ah no. *(Putting helmet on and off.)* Ah no. I was looking for Jim. Is he home?

OLD MAN: Jim who? There's no Jim here?

VISITOR: Jim...Jim...It'll come to me in a minute. Ah, I dunno. Jim. *(Shaking helmet.)* Is this thing not workin'... Will ye not be watching the match? *(He puts helmet on.)* Does this thing work? *(He takes it off.)* Does it not work?

JODY: Sure there's no power. The...you know...crisis..

VISITOR: Crisis? Hah?

OLD MAN: Jesus, where have you been? Isn't the whole world on the brink?

VISITOR: Brink? How d'ya mean "brink"?

JODY: You know. The alert.

(VISITOR *looks puzzled.*)

VISITOR: *(Remembering)* Ah...sure that's over this ages.

OLD MAN: Over. When?

VISITOR: Ah, weeks ago. Sure it only lasted a couple of days. Didn't it turn out yer sham with the long beard had no lead in his pencil? *(Looks around. Shakes head.)* Ah Jesus, ye're not still...Ah Jesus. That's the best yet.

JODY: But the phones. The power. There's nothing.

VISITOR: The power is back...oh, ages...

OLD MAN: Not here, it's not. Not in this street.

VISITOR: Sure I'm only after coming up from the pub. It's your fuse-box, I'd say. Where is it? *(Replaces helmet on stand.)*

JODY: It's in the hall. (JODY *leads the way out into the hall. Ad-lib mumbling in the hall as they locate the fuse-box and notice the trip-switch is off. Suddenly the lights come on. The* VISITOR *re-enters.)*

VISITOR: There ye'are now. Many hands make light work, as the man said.

(Suddenly realising the helmet is now working, he picks it up and puts it on. A female voice can be heard over gentle piano music. The VISITOR *immediately responds to the 3-D world of the helmet.)*

VISITOR: Ah, hello darlin'. How are thingeens? What have you got to say for yourself? *(The reception starts to break down.)*

FEMALE PRESENTER: Teh..stt...cha..pemp...tah...etc. etc.

VISITOR: *(Taking off helmet and shaking it vigorously.)* Is she missin'?

JODY: What?

VISITOR: She's inclined to misfire a bit, I'd say. Sez you, I wouldn't mind firin' your wan there, hah! I'd fire her engine for her. Hah?

JODY: *(Indicating the antennae on the helmet.)* These bloody things aren't working properly.

VISITOR: Not at all. It's nothing to do with that gizmo.

JODY: What is it so?

VISITOR: It's your earth. That's where yer problem is.

JODY: Earth? What so you mean "earth"?

VISITOR: You need a decent earth on a yoke like that. It's not sufficiently earthed.

JODY: Sure isn't there an earth on the plug.

VISITOR: No good. You need a separate earth on a yoke like that. Your normal household earth is no use. *(Aside to* OLD MAN.*)* Too subject to fluctuations in the weather.

JODY: Weather? What in the name of God has the weather to do with it?

VISITOR: Oh a lot. I remember years ago the local radio station used to drift up and down the wave-band because of the weather. *(He goes to* OLD MAN.*)* The fine weather causes the earth to dry up. Unless you keep the earth wet, your signal won't stay put in the one place. I heard me father telling the man who ran the radio station...He was an electrician, me father...He could do anything. Sparks, they called him.

OLD MAN: You wouldn't be one of the Sparks Clarks, would you?

VISITOR: Ah no...no. Anyway, he said to them, throw a couple of buckets of water on your earth rod every morning. It never budged from that day on.

JODY: You're joking.

VISITOR: I'm not. That fecken aerial is no good. It's only an ornament. It's earth you want.

JODY: Well, we have plenty of that here. *(Slaps wardrobe.)*

(FEMALE PRESENTER's *voice comes clearly over the helmet.)*

FEMALE PRESENTER: And soon we'll be going over to our commentator for the opening of today's long-awaited tussle.

VISITOR: Jaze, I better make tracks, as the fellah said..

OLD MAN: Who's this Jim you were lookin' for anyway?

VISITOR: Oh, yeah. Jim...Jim...Jim Forde. Yeah, that's it.

OLD MAN: I'm John Forde. Is it me you're looking for?

VISITOR: John Forde. No, that's not it. Jim...Jim...No...wait a minute now.

JODY: Jody? Jody Forde?

VISITOR: Yeah, that's it. Jody Forde.

JODY: I'm Jody Forde.

VISITOR: Oh, right, How' ya doin'. *(Stretches out hand and shakes hands with* JODY.*)* Pleased to meet you. I have a message. *(Searches in pockets.)* I wrote it down. It's from Pat. Pat...Pat... y'know? She wants you to ring her. She can't get through. Is yer phone out of order?

(JODY *looks at telephone and then at* OLD MAN.)

VISITOR: Ha, ha. Did ye not pay the bill? Them boys don't let the grass grow.

JODY: How did you come to know her?

VISITOR: I'm a friend of Simon's — her...you know *(Gives a knowing wink)*...fella. She wants you to ring her. She gave me directions. We were headin' down this way anyways for the match.

JODY: Who?

VISITOR: Oh meself and Simon and his young fella.

JODY: What young fella?

VISITOR: She wants you to ring her. You were supposed to ring. Are you her brother or something?

JODY: What young fella?

VISITOR: Young Dylan. Simon's lad. We came down for the match. *(To* OLD MAN.*)* Nice young fella. A bit quiet. But we'll make a man of him.

JODY: Where are they now?

VISITOR: In the pub. Drinkin' pints. Havin' the crack. Sure you have to have the crack. *(Waves scarf and leaps around.)* Ole ole ole ole...

JODY: *(Insistently)* What pub?

VISITOR: I dunno. Down by the ground. Why? What's it to you?

JODY: *(Shouts.)* What fucking pub?

VISITOR: Wha? Jesus, there's no call for that kind of language. Mooney's, I think.

(JODY *looks to* OLD MAN, *then rushes out.* VISITOR, *after a moment's pause, makes a move for the bottle of wine, but is interrupted by* JODY's *re-entry. He picks up the accordion instead.* JODY *goes to wardrobe and dons the* OLD MAN's *long black coat.* OLD MAN *looks at him sardonically.*)

JODY: Well, it's raining. (JODY *exits.* VISITOR *begins to play* 'The Dawning of the Day' *on the accordion.* OLD MAN *descends on him and glares.*)

OLD MAN: If there's music in Hell!

BLACKOUT.

END OF PLAY.